Blue Tassels

45 Devotions for the
Desperate, Determined, and Delivered

DEBBIE ROTH

©2024 by Debbie Roth. All rights reserved

Unless otherwise noted, Scripture quotations are taken from *Holy Bible*, New International Version, NIV, Copyright ©1973, 1978, 1984, 2011 by Biblica, Inc. Used by permission. All rights reserved worldwide.

Scripture quotations noted (ESV) are taken from *The Holy Bible*, English Standard Version, ESV, Copyright © 2001 by Crossway Bibles, a publishing ministry of Good News Publishers. All rights reserved.

Scripture quotations noted (NLT) are taken from *Holy Bible*, New Living Translation, NLT, Copyright ©1996, 2004, 2015 by Tyndale House Foundation. Used by permission of Tyndale House Publishers, Inc., Carol Stream, Illinois 60188. All rights reserved.

Cover design by Debbie Roth

ISBN: 978-1-963611-37-3

Published by EA Books Publishing, a division of Living Parables of Central Florida, Inc. a 501c3
EABooksPublishing.com

Dewey

Thank you for listening to God's voice at a time when I was desperate. Thank you for being my original tassel before I was able to reach out to the tassel of Jesus Christ.

TABLE OF CONTENTS

Foreword 1

TASSEL OF COMPASSION 5

   Desperation→Compassion 6

   Father and Son.. 10

   Jesus Felt, Jesus Fed 14

   Oh, Lord, Help Me... 18

   Sharing the Tassel of Compassion................ 22

TASSEL OF HOPE 27

   Desperation→Determination→Hope 28

   Persevering in the Promises.......................... 32

   Confident Assurance 36

   God Giving His ALL/Me Giving My ALL......40

   Sharing the Tassel of Hope: Holding Onto Promises Empowers 44

TASSEL OF STRENGTH 49

   Determination→Strength.............................. 50

   A Splash in the Face.. 54

 The Choice, the Chance, the Change 59
 Strength for Today, Bright Hope
 for Tomorrow 63
 Sharing the Tassel of Strength 67

TASSEL OF COMFORT 71
 Determination→Delivered→Comfort 72
 Even Jesus 76
 Comforted by Friends 80
 Washed Whiter Than Snow 84
 Sharing the Tassel of Comfort 88

TASSEL OF RELATIONSHIP 93
 Determined→Deliverance→Relationship 94
 Fixing Our Eyes on Jesus 96
 Lord, I Want to See 101
 The Good Shepherd 105
 Sharing the Tassel of Relationship 108

TASSEL OF LOVE 113
 Determined→Deliverance→Love 114
 Sensing the Savior 118
 Love Language 122
 Inner Strength 126
 Sharing the Tassel of Love 130

TASSEL OF FORGIVENESS 133
- Delivered→Forgiveness 134
- Freedom Within 138
- A Slice of Humble Pie 142
- Forgiveness 147
- Sharing the Tassel of Forgiveness 151

TASSEL OF REST 155
- Deliverance→Rest 156
- A Beautiful Mess 160
- A Place of Rest 164
- Beauty in the Singer 168
- Sharing the Tassel of Rest 172

TASSEL OF PEACE 177
- Delivered→Peace 178
- Woman at the Well: Cherished, Caught, Comforted 182
- Peace of God 187
- A Path of Peace 191
- Sharing the Tassel of Peace 195

Afterword 199

A Tassel of Thanks 203

About the Author 205

Foreword

JESUS GOT INTO THE boat again and went back to the other side of the lake, where a large crowd gathered around him on the shore. Then a leader of the local synagogue, whose name was Jairus, arrived. When he saw Jesus, he fell at his feet, pleading fervently with him. "My little daughter is dying," he said. "Please come and lay your hands on her; heal her so she can live."

Jesus went with him, and all the people followed, crowding around him. A woman in the crowd had suffered for twelve years with constant bleeding. She had suffered a great deal from many doctors, and over the years she had spent everything she had to pay them, but she had gotten no better. In fact, she had gotten worse. She had heard about Jesus, so she came up behind him through the crowd and touched his robe. For she thought to herself, "If I can just touch his robe, I will be healed." Immediately the bleeding stopped, and she could feel in her body that she had been healed of her terrible condition.

Jesus realized at once that healing power had gone out from him, so he turned around in the crowd and asked, "Who touched my robe?"

His disciples said to him, "Look at this crowd pressing around you. How can you ask, 'Who touched me?'"

But he kept on looking around to see who had done it. Then the frightened woman, trembling at the realization of what had happened to her, came and fell to her knees in front of him and told him what she had done. And he said to her, "Daughter, your faith has made you well. Go in peace. Your suffering is over." (Mark 5:21-34 NLT)

You are about to spend nine weeks immersed in the desperation, determination, and deliverance of this unnamed woman who reached out in faith and experienced a life-changing miracle.

Why *Blue Tassels*?

Mark wrote that the woman "touched his robe." Luke said it was "the fringe of his robe." According to an interview with Rabbi Jason Sobel ("A Miracle 450 Years in the Making" https://www.youtube.com/watch?v=WRpGce4nEFA), it was the tzitzit, the ritual, blue-threaded tassels commanded in Numbers 15:37-41 to be placed on the hems of every four-cornered garment.

The interesting thing is that the woman could have been fulfilling a Messianic prophecy when she reached out for healing by touching the tassels. Malachi 4:2 (NLT) says "But for you who fear my name, the Sun of Righteousness will rise with healing in his wings." Of course, that only becomes significant when you learn that the Hebrew word for *wings* is the same word used for the four corners of a traditional garment.

Rabbi Sobel: "So, the corners of the garment, which the fringes are on, are connected to the Messiah, who is the Sun of Righteousness, who's going to rise up with healing in his wings. So when she touches the hem of his garment, obviously she finds a fulfillment of that verse in his life because she finds the healing that's in him and she's transformed."

Nine Blue Tassels of Transformation

In the following pages, you will find five days' worth of thoughts about each of nine attributes that Debbie calls you to meditate on, pray about, and be transformed by. Each day ends with some Scripture "threads" for you to follow up on and space for you to record your reactions and prayers.

Maybe you find yourself in a desperate place.

Maybe these devotions can help you stir up a determination to reach out and touch the tassels on the robe of Jesus.

Maybe your deliverance is just around the corner.

Dewey Roth
April 2024
P.S.: Stick around for the end of Jairus' story in the *Afterword*.

WEEK ONE

TASSEL OF COMPASSION

Blue Tassels

DAY 1

Desperation→Compassion

Mark 5:21-24 (NLT)

JESUS GOT INTO THE boat again and went back to the other side of the lake, where a large crowd gathered around him on the shore. Then a leader of the local synagogue, whose name was Jairus, arrived. When he saw Jesus, he fell at his feet, pleading fervently with him. "My little daughter is dying," he said. "Please come and lay your hands on her; heal her so she can live."

Jesus went with him, and all the people followed, crowding around him.

TASSEL OF COMPASSION

Have you ever been in a desperate, tearful, fearful, pleading place where urgency was foremost in your mind?

I am sure my father was in that desperate place when I ran through a glass panel of a back door in our garage and then attempted to retreat, causing a major injury to my wrist. Only four years old, I don't remember his reaction, only that he suddenly appeared at the screen door connecting the house to the garage.

After he frantically called on the neighbor who was a nurse, my only memory takes me to the back seat of the car and her squeezing my arm tight as a tourniquet. My dad knew that time was important. He needed to get me to a hospital as soon as possible.

Within the pressing crowd on the narrow streets, Jairus saw Jesus. He dropped to his knees, acknowledging the healing power of this man of God in a submissive and humble posture, and pleaded earnestly for his touch to heal his very sick daughter.

Jairus had left his dying daughter's side to seek Jesus. He had faith and put his full trust in Jesus, and yet knew that time was of the essence. Jesus, with compassion and intention and the crowd pressing in and around him, went with Jairus.

Jesus' reputation preceded him. He showed compassion to men, women, and children prompting him to feed the masses, heal the sick, restore sight, make the lame walk, and cast out demons. Jesus was and is a compassionate teacher and a gentle shepherd to his sheep, not abandoning us.

Have we waited until a desperate situation comes our way to reach out to our compassionate Father? Are there times when we feel a crowd demanding so much from him that we think, "How would he have time to care for me, too?"

Jesus loves us. He wants us to constantly reach out to him; in desperate situations, in times of grief, and in times of praise. Jesus cares for us deeply with the love of his Father.

Threads

Psalm 95:6; Isaiah 41:10; Hebrews 4:16; Hebrews 11:1

Blue Tassels

DAY 2

Father and Son

John 1:1-2, 14;14:6-7 (NIV); Hebrews 1:3 (NLT)

In the beginning was the Word, and the Word was with God, and the Word was God. He was with God in the beginning. The Word became flesh and made his dwelling among us. We have seen his glory, the glory of the one and only Son, who came from the Father, full of grace and truth.

Jesus answered [his disciples], "I am the way and the truth and the life. No one comes to the Father except through me. If you know me, you will know my Father as well. From now on, you do know him and have seen him.

The Son radiates God's own glory and expresses the very character of God, and he sustains everything by the mighty power of his command. When he had cleansed us from our sins, he sat down in the place of honor at the right hand of the majestic God in heaven.

When we attended our home church (when back in town for a visit), we often heard, "I feel like it's Dewey (my husband) walking through the church again." They were referring to our son, Curtis, when he was just a little tyke. As he grew older, we continued to hear, "He looks just like his dad!"

Curtis now serves as a full-time Children's Pastor at the same church where his dad served four years as a Youth Pastor. Now that Curtis has married and has a family of his own, there are still comments about how much they look and act alike. Both have put their loving, merciful, mighty God first in their lives. Like father, like son.

Do we ever question what God the Father is like? Have we wondered what it would have been like to see Jesus in the flesh? What would it have been like to be in his presence and see his eyes of compassion? Would we have listened intently to his words of wisdom, and experienced seeing the touch of healing?

Jesus was a reflection, the image, of his Father, full of grace and truth. His attributes/character traits reflect his Father in ways of mercy, wisdom, faithfulness, kindness, and graciousness. Jesus is humble, loves unconditionally, and is compassionate. Jesus showed incredible compassion for us when he shed his blood on the cross.

What would you have asked Jesus if you encountered him on the street? Would you be awe-filled, skeptical, curious, thankful, desperate to touch his robe?

We still can encounter Jesus through the Holy Spirit. We can have that relationship with him, reaching in prayer, reading his word, feeling his comfort, finding rest, and living with the hope of eternity with him. Have faith for he is the way, truth, and life.

Threads

Psalm 103:13; Isaiah 49:13; Lamentations 3:22-23

DAY 3

Jesus Felt, Jesus Fed

Matthew 14:14-21 (NLT)

JESUS SAW THE HUGE crowd as he stepped from the boat, and he had compassion on them and healed their sick.

That evening the disciples came to him and said, "This is a remote place, and it's already getting late. Send the crowds away so they can go to the villages and buy food for themselves."

But Jesus said, "That isn't necessary—you feed them."

"But we have only five loaves of bread and two fish!" they answered.

"Bring them here," he said. Then he told the people to sit down on the grass. Jesus took the five loaves and two fish, looked up toward heaven, and blessed them. Then, breaking the loaves into pieces, he gave the bread to the disciples, who distributed it to the people. They all ate as much as they wanted, and afterward, the disciples picked up twelve baskets of leftovers. About 5,000 men were fed that day, in addition to all the women and children!

How many times have we heard stories about people helping others who go through the same difficulties they experienced themselves, whether physical, emotional, financial, or spiritual?

People who have struggled with their physical health, or the health of family members, often become doctors and nurses. Many special education teachers also have a child with a disability, counselors, and caregivers. How many financial planners have had to tackle their own tough money decisions? Servers at food shelves or homeless shelters often have been on the other side of the ladle. Those who share Jesus Christ, such as inspirational authors, speakers, and pastors, most likely have a testimony of their own.

What do they all have in common? Compassion.

Jesus had just gone through a solitary time to grieve over the loss of John the Baptist, who had been beheaded. Upon his return, he sees this huge crowd. John's execution affected Jesus deeply, and yet he showed compassion by not only healing and teaching, but also feeding them physically.

Jesus was experiencing the emotions of grief and sadness over his loss, however, he turned the focus from himself and shifted it to the crowd's needs.

When feeling helpless and drowning in pain, we need to take the focus from ourselves—the suffering, grief, problems, despair, hopelessness, and helplessness—and shift it to Jesus.

We can choose Jesus alone and find beautiful peace and hope in him. That beautiful peace and hope he provides can turn into having compassion for others going through similar difficulties.

God can use your past pain and your present struggles for good. Reach out to him to help you feel the needs around you and to show you how you can minister to those needs with compassion.

Threads

*Psalm 112:1-4; Proverbs 12:25 and 14:21;
Luke 15:20-24; 1 John 3:17-18*

Blue Tassels

DAY 4

Oh, Lord, Help Me

Psalm 86:14-17

ARROGANT FOES ARE ATTACKING me, O God; ruthless people are trying to kill me—they have no regard for you.

But you, Lord, are a compassionate and gracious God, slow to anger, abounding in love and faithfulness.

Turn to me and have mercy on me; show your strength in behalf of your servant; save me, because I serve you just as my mother did.

Give me a sign of your goodness, that my enemies may see it and be put to shame, for you, Lord, have helped me and comforted me.

Desperation is when the pressure is about to blow the lid off! Don't give up!

Maybe you have been through an awful event in your life, possibly seeing the light at the end of the tunnel, but the experience has left you wondering and playing the soundtrack over and over again. How did you make it through? My first guess is that someone helped you amid the pain.

Maybe it has been a health issue, possibly heart or cancer. Maybe it has been a major financial loss or the loss of a home due to a natural disaster. Maybe it has been death, a miscarriage, or the devastating loss of a loved one. Possibly even a marriage on the rocks or a difficult situation with a child.

Emotional pain could have come from a betrayal, abuse, or divorce. Internal emotional pain could also be caused by our making wrong choices against God's will (i.e., sin).

Earlier in Psalm 86 (a prayer of David), David acknowledges God's forgiveness, love, greatness, faithfulness, graciousness, strength, and compassion. Throughout the psalm, David also declares his dependence on God, saying that he is the only God.

David trusts him, calls to him in his distress because God answers, praising him for his greatness and marvelous deeds, and he will glorify his name forever. David acknowledges God has delivered him from the depths and realm of the dead, and has provided him with help and comfort.

Blue Tassels

When you pray to God, do you first give him adoration, praising him for things he has done in your life? We tend to ask for this, plead for that, "please make this happen," but forget to first acknowledge the things he has provided in our lives.

Praising him first lets him know how much we love and trust him and are thankful for what he has done.

Threads

Psalm 34:18; Psalm 36

DAY 5

Sharing the Tassel of Compassion
Luke 10:30-36 (ESV)

Jesus replied, "A man was going down from Jerusalem to Jericho, and he fell among robbers, who stripped him and beat him and departed, leaving him half dead.

"Now by chance a priest was going down that road and when he saw him he passed by on the other side. So likewise a Levite, when he came to the place and saw him, passed by on the other side.

"But a Samaritan, as he journeyed, came to where he was, and when he saw him, he had compassion. He went to him and bound up his wounds, pouring on oil and wine. Then he set him on his own animal and brought him to an inn and took care of him. And the next day he took out two denarii and gave them to the innkeeper, saying, 'Take care of him, and whatever more you spend, I will repay you when I come back.'

"Which of these three, do you think, proved to be a neighbor to the man who fell among the robbers?"

He said, "The one who showed him mercy."

And Jesus said to him, "You go, and do likewise."

Our scripture for today is Jesus' response to the question, "Who is my neighbor?"

After the priest and Levite pass by without helping, the Samaritan has compassion upon the injured victim. Culturally, the Samaritan should not have helped the Jew, but he chose to act on his compassion and help the man, not only physically, but helping with money for extended care. So, maybe the question should be, "How can I help my neighbor?"

Sometimes we find ourselves in situations where we notice a need, we see someone struggling and wish we had the strength to help somehow. It might just be that they needed a listening ear, a twenty-second hug, a word of encouragement, or a tissue. They may be looking for someone they can trust or someone who would show kindness. In a more tangible way, they might need a vehicle to borrow temporarily, a ride to an appointment, a gift card with which to buy groceries until the next paycheck comes in.

Ask God to show you when, where, and how to show compassion to your "neighbor."

Sometimes, it's easier to notice the "neighbor" than it is ourselves. Are there times when we might need to show ourselves compassion?

We often hear, "Forgive those, as we have been forgiven." Do we hear, "Show compassion, as we have been shown compassion?"

Blue Tassels

Ask and trust God to provide compassion, hope, strength, comfort, love, forgiveness, rest, and peace. Then we will be ready to show compassion to our "neighbor." Compassion leads to action.

Threads

Ephesians 4:32; Colossians 3:12; 1 Peter 3:8

WEEK TWO

TASSEL OF HOPE

Blue Tassels

DAY 1

Desperation→Determination→Hope

Mark 5:25-27 (NLT)

A WOMAN IN THE crowd had suffered for twelve years with constant bleeding. She had suffered a great deal from many doctors, and over the years she had spent everything she had to pay them, but she had gotten no better. In fact, she had gotten worse. She had heard about Jesus, so she came up behind him through the crowd and touched his robe.

Today, we find ourselves in the middle of another story. Jesus and the twelve disciples had returned to Capernaum and were met with a large crowd. A synagogue leader, Jairus, saw Jesus and publicly pled at his feet to come to his house to heal his dying twelve-year-old daughter.

On the way, a woman who had been bleeding for twelve years stopped him in his tracks. We move from Jairus pleading to a woman bleeding; from Jairus wanting Jesus' touch to heal his daughter to a woman wanting to touch Jesus to be healed.

Words in this passage that stand out: suffered, constant, spent everything, no better, worse.

For twelve years she had suffered physically, emotionally, financially, relationally, and spiritually. She was exhausted, weak, shamed, and an outcast because of being unclean (Leviticus 15:25-28). Her finances were spent searching for a cure that never happened. She was most likely isolated and rejected because of her disease. She had no relief, as the condition was constant.

She was desperate, but also determined. She had heard about Jesus. Possible thoughts of the woman: "If only I could touch Him, the man who I heard healed others. I must do whatever I can to secretly touch just the edge of his robe, to not make him unclean, and that others may not see me."

I can only imagine when she spotted Jesus, everything around her became blurred. Her focus was on that robe. She did not care about anyone or anything else but knew that touching the clothing of Jesus would heal. Persistence is the word that comes to mind. She was persistent in staying on course and making her way through the crowd, even with the possibility of being found out, publicly ridiculed, and spoken to harshly.

Have there been events in your life when you have felt shamed or rejected by family and/or friends? Has there been an instance when you needed to reach out for some financial help? What about doubting God, but not wanting anyone to know, so you just keep going through the motions of having a great spiritual life?

You, too, can reach out and touch the tassel of hope on the edge of Jesus' robe. Ask him to show you the truth and the hope that only he can provide. Pray for his understanding, his forgiveness, and his guidance. The woman knew she was unclean, but her desperation and determination took her through her fear to reach Jesus. She chose faith over fear and reached for hope.

Threads

Psalm 42; Mark 10:46-52

DAY 2

Persevering in the Promises

Romans 5:1-5

THEREFORE, SINCE WE HAVE been justified through faith, we have peace with God through our Lord Jesus Christ, through whom we have gained access by faith into this grace in which we now stand. And we boast in the hope of the glory of God. Not only so, but we also glory in our sufferings, because we know that suffering produces perseverance; perseverance, character; and character, hope. And hope does not put us to shame, because God's love has been poured out into our hearts through the Holy Spirit, who has been given to us.

On March 11, 2024, the last person living in an iron lung due to polio passed away, after relying on the iron lung for 70 years. During that time, he graduated from high school and college, went to law school and passed the bar exam, became a successful lawyer, and in 2020 wrote a book about his experience. A quote from a longtime friend said he was a driven man with a strong faith in God.*

Suffering produced perseverance; perseverance, character; and character, hope.

Often our lives seem to be stagnant; suffering through abuse, betrayal, disease, financial problems, and depression. Will these sufferings end? Faith has been shaky at times and hope has wavered, but with perseverance, steps of transformation have only built up my character and belief in the promise of hope.

Have there been day-after-day struggles in your life when you thought they would never end? Tomorrow and the next day and the next seem the same and your strength wanes, the tunnel looks longer and darker, and there seems to be no way out.

But Jesus is our, HOPE. Yes! Hope in him will not lead to disappointment because we know that "God's love has been poured out into our hearts through the Holy Spirit!" (Romans 5:5)

The woman bleeding for twelve years persevered. She was desperate and determined to get to the end of the horrible suffering in her life. Though we don't read it in our scripture, I can imagine there were times she wanted to give up, feeling hopeless, believing there was no end in sight.

Persevere and lean on Jesus. He's waiting to hear from you. He will take your suffering, help you persevere, strengthen your character, and provide you with hope; leading you to confidence in him. May we all persevere to live in his promises.

"God's delays are not His denials. If you're in a season of waiting, please know you are not the only one. Hold on to hope, my friend. God sees. He knows. He loves you!" (Cindy Bultema)

*"Texas Man Who Used an Iron Lung for Decades after Contracting Polio as a Child Dies at 78," today.com, March 13, 2024, https://www.today.com/health/news/man-iron-lung-polio-dies-paul-alexander-rcna143318.

Threads

Colossians 1:27, 1 Peter 1:3-7

Blue Tassels

DAY 3

Confident Assurance

Hebrews 11:1

NOW FAITH IS CONFIDENCE in what we hope for and assurance about what we do not see.

Whenever asked in a "get to know you" game what animal I would want to be, my answer was a bird. Flying in the sky seemed so freeing and beautiful, enjoying God's creation from the air, out in the open.

For my 50th birthday, my husband surprised me with a greeting card with a picture of a skydiver on the front. What? Yes, I went skydiving. Part of the orientation was a video on the procedures and signing a document stating you understood you could die. That was a bit scary, but I signed it anyway.

What I needed was the hope and faith that the instructor had correctly packed my parachute, so that when the cord was pulled, we would float safely to the ground. I needed to have confidence in the instructor I would be attached to and the assurance that the parachute was indeed packed correctly.

Just as my faith in my instructor led me to trust that we would be safe, faith in God leads me to trust in his promises and ability to care for and protect me.

Have we continually trusted in his unfailing love, kindness, grace, forgiveness, mercy, and gentleness? How about hearing my cries, relief from stress, and helping me dwell in safety? (Psalm 4) That trust and confidence leads to faith.

Faith is needed when our senses cannot see or touch him. In faith, we can reach out to God in prayer. Hebrews 10:23 says "Let us hold unswervingly to the hope we profess, for he who promised is faithful."

The bleeding woman had confidence enough to find her way through the busy street that was crowded with those who were curious and squeezing their way through to see this man called Jesus.

Believe today. Have faith. Have the confidence in what you hope for and the assurance about what you cannot see. Trust that he loves you no matter what. Trust his character. He is there. He is listening. He cares for you. "Blessed assurance, Jesus is mine!" (Fanny Crosby)

Threads

Psalm 62:5-8; Hebrews 12

DAY 4

God Giving His ALL/Me Giving My ALL

John 3:16-17 (NLT)

FOR THIS IS HOW God loved the world: He gave his one and only Son, so that everyone who believes in him will not perish but have eternal life. God sent his Son into the world not to judge the world, but to save the world through him.

Romans 15:13 (ESV)

May the God of hope fill you with all joy and peace in believing, so that by the power of the Holy Spirit you may abound in hope.

When recording my second CD on hope, I was in Studio A, the large studio with high windows that provide beautiful natural light. While recording, the producer, sitting in another room and able to hear me, stopped the music in my headphones, and said, "Debbie, I can't hear the hope in your voice." Just as an actor on a stage needs to have a louder voice and bigger motions, a singer recording in a studio needs to show the emotion of the song through the voice. I lifted my eyes to God's beauty through the window and gave my all to allow hope to be imparted to the listeners.

God gives his **ALL**: Adoration, Loyalty, and Longevity.

Adoration

The Psalms are full of God's adoration and love toward us. He lavishes us with his love (1 John 3:1), and his love is unfailing and endures forever. He gave his one and only son to die for our sins so that we would not perish, but have everlasting life. Greater love has no one than this: to lay down one's life for one's friends. (John 15:13)

Loyalty

God is loyal. Nothing can separate us from God's loyalty, love, and faithfulness. (Romans 8:38-39)

Longevity

The steadfast love of the Lord never ceases; his mercies never come to an end; they are new every morning; great is your faithfulness. (Lamentations 3:22-23) His kingdom is an everlasting kingdom, and his dominion endures through all generations. The Lord is trustworthy in all he promises and faithful in all he does. (Psalm 145:13)

The bleeding woman gave everything she had within her to touch his robe and be healed. She was focused. She gave up knowing she was unclean and may be making others unclean as well. She had the hope that if she gave everything she had, she would be healed. She gave her **ALL** at the moment of touch.

How can we give our **ALL**? Praise the Lord through worship, commit our way to him, seek him daily through prayer and scripture, and continue to press on toward the goal of winning the prize for which God has called us heavenward in Christ Jesus. (Philippians 3:14)

Threads

Psalm 73:26; Psalm 95:6-7;
1 Thessalonians 5:16; Hebrews 12:2

Blue Tassels

DAY 5

Sharing the Tassel of Hope
Holding **O**nto **P**romises **E**mpowers
Psalm 33:20-22 (NLT)

WE PUT OUR HOPE in the Lord. He is our help and our shield.

In him our hearts rejoice, for we trust in his holy name.

Let your unfailing love surround us, Lord, for our hope is in you alone.

> Standing on the promises of Christ, my King,
> Through eternal ages let his praises ring;
> Glory in the highest, I will shout and sing,
> Standing on the promises of God.
>> *Russell Kelso Carter (1886), Public Domain*

In the hymn, *Standing on the Promises*, I love the lyric, "I will shout and sing."

Had the bleeding woman heard of the promises of God? We don't know exactly what she heard about Jesus. What stories had she heard about the promises of Jesus healing people? Had she been a witness to someone receiving the touch from Jesus and being healed?

I have an "amplified" version of the acronym for which this day's thought is titled. **H**olding **o**nto (grasping hold of) God's **p**romises (His assurances for our life), **e**mpowers (strengthens, and equips us).

Holding onto: grasping hold of, hanging onto, owning, treasuring, believing. David says, "I keep my eyes always on the Lord. With him at my right hand, I will not be shaken." (Psalm 16:8) James writes, "Blessed is the one who perseveres under trial because, having stood the test, that person will receive the crown of life that the Lord has promised to those who love him." (James 1:12)

Promises: God's assurances, binding declarations for our life throughout his word. God promises to give rest to those who come to him.

(Matthew 11:28-30) Those who mourn will be comforted. (Matthew 5:4) He tells us not to be afraid, for he gives us peace. (John 14:27) Rest, peace, strength, power, perseverance, and eternal life, are only a few of God's promises.

Empowers: God strengthens. He equips us. We benefit from the power of the same spirit that raised Christ from the dead! (Romans 8:11)

In Psalm 16:8, David says, "I keep my eyes always on the Lord. With him at my right hand, I will not be shaken."

Rest, peace, power, perseverance, and eternal life are only a few of God's promises.

Have you grasped hold of and believed in God's promises for yourself? If so, glory in the highest! Shout and sing about the hope that lives within you.

Threads

Psalm 16:8; Matthew 11:28-30;
John 14:27; Romans 8:11

WEEK THREE

TASSEL OF STRENGTH

Blue Tassels

DAY 1

Determination→Strength

Mark 5:28 (NLT)

FOR SHE THOUGHT TO herself, "If I can just touch his robe, I will be healed."

Have you heard of if-then statements? A **conditional statement** (also called an if-then statement) is a statement with a hypothesis followed by a conclusion. The hypothesis is the first, or "if," part of a conditional statement. The conclusion is the second, or "then," part of a conditional statement. The conclusion is the result of a hypothesis.*

If you practice your spelling words, *then* you can play outside.

If it snows enough, *then* school will be canceled.

If I get to the airport late, *then* I may miss my flight.

If you trust in the Lord with all your heart and lean not on your own understanding; in all your ways submit to him *then* he will make your paths straight. (Proverbs 3:5-6)

If you seek me with all your heart, *then* you will find me. (Jeremiah 29:13)

Having heard about Jesus, the woman thought, "*If* I could just touch his robe, *then* I will be healed." Her conditional statement was full of belief, strength, and hope. She hoped she could touch his robe, and believed that if she did, she would be healed.

Her strength (in spite of her physical weakness), determination, and expectation of what Jesus could provide are what got her to that place; to that narrow street in Capernaum crowded with bodies pressing up against each other.

She knew she had to try to avoid touching people (including Jesus) because of being unclean, and when she did touch his garment, attention would most likely be drawn to her. She could be publicly ridiculed and yelled at for being present among the crowd. She probably didn't even know she was interrupting the journey to Jairus' home to care for his dying daughter.

There are times in our lives when we say, "*If only . . . then* maybe . . ." Maybe those thoughts are directed at God during times of pain or desperation. But there was no "maybe" in the woman's thoughts.

We too can have determination and strength to reach out in prayer through Jesus Christ. Our hearts can have the expectation and assurance shown in her thought: "I will be healed."

What *if/then* questions or statements have you brought before God? Pray believing. *When I . . . then He.*

* "If Then Statements," K12.LibreTexts.org, https://k12.libretexts.org/Bookshelves/Mathematics/Geometry/02%3A_Reasoning_and_Proof/2.11%3A_If_Then_Statements.

Threads

John 4:6-8, Matthew 6:14-15, Ephesians 3:16-19

Blue Tassels

DAY 2

A Splash in the Face

Psalm 59:16-17

BUT I WILL SING of your strength, in the morning I will sing of your love; for you are my fortress, my refuge in times of trouble.

You are my strength, I sing praise to you; you, God, are my fortress, my God on whom I can rely.

Are you an early bird or a night owl? Do you go to bed at a decent time for your wonderful, restful sleep and wake up refreshed? The reflection in the mirror shows someone rested, confident, and strong ready to tackle their day.

Or, like me, do you watch the 10 or 11 pm news, not set an alarm, and wake up the next morning . . . with crusty eyes and the mirror showing a reflection of someone with little sleep, plenty of stress, and a bit of weakness to start their day?

Whether an early bird or a night owl, restful sleep can be stolen by a disturbing dream. Maybe a restless sleep was caused by thoughts of past circumstances, present-day schedules, or future plans that haven't quite been set.

Past circumstances, present schedules, and plans for the future: Can you carry all of those yourself? I sure can't.

The woman most likely woke up to another day of bleeding. Her past circumstances have overcome her for 12 years. Her day possibly begins with pain, exhaustion (even after sleeping), knowing she is still unclean, and having no friends or family to reach out to.

What kind of schedule will she have today, knowing she'll need to avoid people? Does she have a tomorrow? Her desperation in trying to survive and find hope in her horrible situation leads to a determination to have faith in healing, and finding the strength it will take to get through another day. My guess is that kind of attitude helped her wake up with strength in her body and mind, wipe her eyes, and start a new day!

In the morning we can splash water on our face, refreshing it for our day, reminding ourselves of God's love and that he is our fortress, our refuge in times of trouble, our strength and one whom we can rely upon.

We can clear those crusty eyes! "I finally threw in the towel. But God threw it back and said, 'Wipe your face girl. We're almost there.'"*

By giving gratitude to God for getting us through yesterday and waking us up today, our attitude can change. Our reflection in the mirror can begin to exude freshness and faith that God will be with us. Take time to be still, pray, allow him to carry your burdens, and be thankful. Focus on him and he will provide strength for whatever comes your way. (1 Thessalonians 5:16-17)

When our attitude changes, our behaviors will begin to change. Take time to sing a song to the Lord, play praise music, or ask God to show you someone that needs encouragement. Think of the senses that God gave you and ask him to show you how you can use your hands, feet, eyes, and ears to touch, travel, see, and hear what good work he has planned for you that day. (Psalm 34:8; Psalm 143:8-10)

In the morning, splash water on your face and thank God for his strength for the day.

* Kelly's Treehouse, Facebook post.

Threads

2 Samuel 22:33; Psalm 46:1;
Matthew 11:28-30;1 Peter 5:7-10

DAY 3

The Choice, the Chance, the Change

Proverbs 3:3-6, 21-22

LET LOVE AND FAITHFULNESS never leave you; bind them around your neck, write them on the tablet of your heart. Then you will win favor and a good name in the sight of God and man.

Trust in the Lord with all your heart and lean not on your own understanding; in all your ways submit to him and he will make your paths straight.

My son, do not let wisdom and understanding out of your sight, preserve sound judgment and discretion; they will be life for you, an ornament to grace your neck.

Blue Tassels

Once upon a time, there was a nineteen-year-old, broken-down, confused girl. Through a few circumstances, she ended up being chosen to act in a community theatre's production of a musical comedy called *Godspell*. She had no idea what it was about, but it was a way to distract herself from her current, less-than-wonderful, situation.

Also cast in this play was a man who loved Jesus. Through their conversations, he helped her see how God loved her and how important the Lord would be in her life. The choice to audition for the play was difficult, and the choice to share her story and develop a friendship with this man made her feel vulnerable.

The girl took the chance to follow Jesus, who took her under the shelter of his wings and showed her a strength she didn't know she had, warmth of compassion, comfort, love, and, most of all, hope for eternity.

The change in her life has not always been easy. She has had questions: Why was I abused? Why did I get cancer? Why this or that? But God has always been there for her.

If you haven't guessed by now, she . . . is me, and yes, I not only became the bride of Jesus, but became the compassionate man's wife.

Choosing to take the chance so your life might change can be scary. The bleeding woman chose to show up on that road at that time, knowing Jesus would be there. Knowing the condemnation that could come from the crowd, she had the strength of will to find her way to Jesus. She had the confidence that if she touched the robe, she would be healed. Her life would be changed.

Is there a choice you need to make? Is it surrendering your life to Christ? Or if you have already made a decision to follow him, has the road been tough and you need to make a choice to return to him?

Be strong and courageous and take the chance. Had the bleeding woman not acted on her courage to take the chance, use the strength it took to get to him, and act in the faith that he would heal her, her life may have never been changed.

Choose to trust in the Lord, submit to him, and he will change your life and make your paths straight.

Threads

Psalm 16:1-2; 1 Peter 1:6-9

DAY 4

Strength for Today, Bright Hope for Tomorrow

Isaiah 40:28-31

DO YOU NOT KNOW? Have you not heard? The Lord is the everlasting God, the Creator of the ends of the earth. He will not grow tired or weary, and his understanding no one can fathom. He gives strength to the weary and increases the power of the weak. Even youths grow tired and weary, and young men stumble and fall; but those who hope in the Lord will renew their strength. They will soar on wings like eagles; they will run and not grow weary, they will walk and not be faint.

Blue Tassels

You may recognize the words of today's title from a verse in a popular hymn, *Great Is Thy Faithfulness.*

> Pardon for sin and a peace that endureth,
> Thine own dear presence to cheer and to guide,
> Strength for today and bright hope for tomorrow
> Blessings all mine, with ten thousand beside!
> *Thomas O. Chisholm/William Runyan (1923) Public Domain*

Our scripture today reminds me of this beautiful verse in the hymn above. Both remind me of the story of Ruth, a small book in the Old Testament of the Bible.

Ruth was a daughter-in-law of Naomi, whose husband and two sons left their homeland because of drought, and settled in the land of Moab. Ruth, a Moabite, married one of the sons. Naomi's husband and both sons died and left the women without husbands. When the drought ended, Naomi traveled back to her homeland, and Ruth followed.

Ruth loved God, had the strength to leave, and was loyal to Naomi. Ruth's strength is shown throughout the book and she is considered a woman of noble character. The hope for tomorrow? Ruth marries Boaz (a relative of Naomi's), and their son is Obed, the grandson of David.

She is one of five women listed in the genealogy of Jesus (Matthew 1:1-17).

Ruth was strong, persistent, compassionate, humble, and trusted God. She was also a widow, had no children, left her home and moved to another country, and worked many hours to provide for Naomi and herself. Through it all, she seemed to soar on wings like eagles, run and not grow weary, and stayed strong.

Is there a road you have traveled or are walking on today that has left you weary and weak, not understanding where God was or is? God is still there, watching you, loving you every step of the way. His love never ceases and his mercies never come to an end. Strength and hope? He replenishes every morning. Those who hope in the Lord will renew their strength.

Threads

Book of Ruth; Psalm 29:11

DAY 5

Sharing the Tassel of Strength
2 Thessalonians 2:16-17; 3:3-5

May our Lord Jesus Christ himself and God our Father, who loved us and by his grace gave us eternal encouragement and good hope, encourage your hearts and strengthen you in every good deed and word.

But the Lord is faithful, and he will strengthen you and protect you from the evil one. We have confidence in the Lord that you are doing and will continue to do the things that we command. May the Lord direct your hearts into God's love and Christ's perseverance.

If you have ever served on a mission trip, you probably have found out that a lot of strength is needed.

Emotionally, we see and feel the needs of those we are serving. Physically, we are needed to help construct walls, paint, pour cement, and travel long distances. Sometimes relationships among the mission workers get tested, usually due to weariness.

During a mission trip to Panama, we traveled to a remote village in the Atlantic Ocean. As in a lot of the villages, resources were sparse. When we arrived the families we were there to serve wanted to make us a meal. When the missionary we were working with was asked how it was possible to eat in front of them when they gave so much of what they had to feed us, his reply was, "If you don't keep up your strength and energy, you won't be able to minister to their needs."

The same is true for all of us. In our scripture today, Paul was encouraging the church in Thessalonica to stand firm against those who have not believed the truth.

Helping others takes endurance, standing firm in the Lord and his protection. May the Lord give you strength, and direct your heart with the Father's love and Christ's perseverance as you reach out to help others.

Threads

Romans 10:14-15; Philippians 3:13-14

WEEK FOUR

TASSEL OF COMFORT

Blue Tassels

DAY 1

Determination→Delivered→Comfort

Mark 5:29 (NLT)

IMMEDIATELY THE BLEEDING STOPPED, and she could feel in her body that she had been healed of her terrible condition.

TASSEL OF COMFORT

Comfort for me has a warm, loving, and calming essence. As a verb, it can mean to soothe, calm, or alleviate pain whether it is physical, emotional, or relational. As a noun, comfort is a condition of contentment, a person or thing bringing consolation, or balm.

As we age, our comforts change. Or do they? What about finding comfort in a special blanket, stuffed animal, real animal, favorite pillow, or your treasured easy chair? As for a state of being calm and relaxed, reading a well-loved book, listening to a song that melts your heart, eating your favorite food, or hearing words of affirmation feed our senses in a way that comforts us.

I cannot imagine how intense the experience of comfort was for the woman in our story when the bleeding suddenly stopped. In that moment of healing, not only was her frail health restored, but also her emotions were calmed, and her relationships would change.

She was no longer unclean, avoided, and shamed. No longer would she be rejected by family and friends. She could be comfortable in her bed covers and her clothing. She now had the freedom to shop in the markets, attend the synagogue, and have heartfelt social conversations. Though we don't read what her future held and what comforting moments she was able to experience, we can assume it was not the same as it had been for the previous twelve years.

What would have happened if her fear had caused her to quietly slip away and not follow through with finding Jesus and touching his robe? Would she have spent the rest of her life confined in her failing health and loneliness?

What we do know is that she believed Jesus could heal her and that he did, right then and there!

There are times when we have fear and trepidation in reaching out to the Lord in times of severe pain, worrisome trials, and intense situations. Will he hear me? Can he heal me? Why, Lord?

Did the woman quietly ask these questions after she heard about others being healed? I believe she did. But her faith won! Through her desperation she became determined. As a result, she was delivered from her ailment; comforted at that moment by Jesus.

Pray, believing that you too can be comforted from any desperation you're feeling. Our prayers are heard!

Threads

Psalm 63:1-8; Jeremiah 29:11-13; Romans 10:17

Blue Tassels

DAY 2

Even Jesus

John 11:35

Jesus wept.

Even though this is the shortest verse in the Bible, it is a very important one. Jesus showed he had emotions.

In Genesis 1:26 we read, "Then God said, 'Let us make mankind in our image, in our likeness . . .'" God created emotions. Jesus experienced the same emotions we endure, such as love and joy (John 15:9-11), sadness and grief (John 11:33-35), anger and frustration (Mark 3:5), and empathy (Hebrews 4:15). Whereas our emotions can lead to sin, Jesus' emotions were without sin and born out of love for his people.

Did you know tears prevent dryness (protect), supply nutrients (feed), provide a smooth surface (comfort), and destroy germs and bacteria (cleanse)? Emotional tears contain feel-good hormones that can diminish physical and emotional pain (soothe). Without tears, we would have irritated and, possibly, scarred eyes.

I can only imagine the woman in our story had cried many tears: tears of pain, tears of loneliness, tears of anger, and/or tears of sadness. Upon hearing that Jesus could heal, seeking him in the crowd, touching the tassel of his robe, and the feeling in her body of healing, those tears of desperation turned to tears of joy, refreshing her weary eyes and converting her tears of pain into tears of praise and thanksgiving for her comfort.

"God didn't promise days without pain, laughter without sorrow, sun without rain, but he did promise strength for the day, comfort for the tears, and light for the way." (unknown)

Reach out to the Lord with your tears of pain, sadness, anger, or loneliness. He will heal and provide comfort. Reach out to the Lord with your tears of joy and praise. He will be joyful with you.

* "The Power of Tears," all-eyes.org, April 21, 2020, https://www.all-eyes.org/the-power-of-tears/.

Threads

Psalm 31; Psalm 56:8; Psalm 147:3

DAY 3

Comforted by Friends

2 Corinthians 7:6-7

But God, who comforts the downcast, comforted us by the coming of Titus, and not only by his coming but also by the comfort you had given him. He told us about your longing for me, your deep sorrow, your ardent concern for me, so that my joy was greater than ever.

God provided comfort through Titus, who might not have been one of Paul's closest friends, but could still give comfort to Paul after a time of no rest and many conflicts. I love that the Corinthians had comforted Titus, shared their concerns about Paul with him, and then Titus was able to share that comfort.

After my mother was placed in a nursing care facility, without the chance of returning to her home, I traveled from Minnesota to Wyoming to clean out her house, preparing it to be put on the market. The days were long, beginning at 6:00 am and usually ending past midnight.

She had collected a multitude of beautifully bound resource books specifically associated with the church she was attending. I knew some parishioners were unable to purchase such books, so I made a call to the pastor to come and pick them up to disperse as he saw fit. When the pastor arrived, he found me tired, depressed, and overwhelmed.

He asked if I knew of Rich Mullins, a Christian singer and musician. "Yes," I replied. He went out to his car and returned with a guitar. He sang a few of Rich's songs. I had never met this man before, but God used this new friend to provide the comfort I needed that day; that very moment.

"As iron sharpens iron, so a friend sharpens a friend." (Proverbs 27:17)

The Bible features many friendships including David and Jonathan (1 Samuel 20:42), Ruth and Naomi (Book of Ruth), and Jesus and his disciples ("Greater love has no one than this: to lay down one's life for one's friends." John 15:13). In all the friendships, the "sharpening" came through mutual comfort, love, encouragement, care, and sacrifice.

I pray that if you do not have a "sharpening" kind of friend, God would provide someone in your life. Remember that Jesus is always present, providing us with comfort, love, encouragement, and care. He sacrificed himself on the cross for you and me. He is a forever friend.

Even in the toughest of times, God provides comfort. He is there in the least expected ways and people. Reach out to him.

Threads

Proverbs 18:24; John 15

DAY 4

Washed Whiter Than Snow

Psalm 51:1-2, 7-12 (NLT)

HAVE MERCY ON ME, O God, because of your unfailing love. Because of your great compassion, blot out the stain of my sins. Wash me clean from my guilt. Purify me from my sin.

Purify me from my sins, and I will be clean; wash me, and I will be whiter than snow. Oh, give me back my joy again; you have broken me—now let me rejoice. Don't keep looking at my sins. Remove the stain of my guilt. Create in me a clean heart, O God. Renew a loyal spirit within me. Do not banish me from your presence, and don't take your Holy Spirit from me.

Restore to me the joy of your salvation, and make me willing to obey you.

"Mercy, love, compassion, blot out the stain of sin, wash me clean from guilt, purify me, give me joy again, let me rejoice, create in me a clean heart, renew a loyal spirit, don't banish me, don't take your Holy Spirit from me, restore joy, make me willing to obey." Wow! Sounds like a beautiful comfort level!

Today's passages were written by King David after he had committed murder and adultery. Nathan, a friend and advisor to David, confronted David. Psalm 51 is a prayer of repentance and a prayer for forgiveness. The discomfort David shares in this psalm includes the stain of his sins and his guilt, rebellion, and brokenness. He prayed to be restored and renewed.

There have been times in my life when I could pray this psalm to God. My mind wanders back to the days of past sins before I knew Jesus. There are moments when current thoughts and actions do not reflect a heart of obedience.

Knowing that our sin is sitting there, and that we have not repented, is very uncomfortable. Discomfort manifests itself in guilt, unforgiveness toward self, brokenness, stress, low self-esteem, and discouragement. Our lives sure don't look like a fresh blanket of snow, but instead resemble muddy waters.

But God! Pray Psalm 51. Repent and ask for forgiveness. Pray for restoration and renewal in your life. Comfort is available in God's mercy, love, compassion, and joy!

Thank you, Lord, for your unfailing love and washing me white as snow!

Threads

Psalm 51

Blue Tassels

DAY 5

Sharing the Tassel of Comfort

2 Corinthians 1:3-4

PRAISE BE TO THE God and Father of our Lord Jesus Christ, the Father of compassion and the God of all comfort, who comforts us in all our troubles, so that we can comfort those in any trouble with the comfort we ourselves receive from God.

TASSEL OF COMFORT

I am at an age when I can look back at my life and realize how God has brought me through the journey to this point. Part of that journey has included abuse, betrayal, death of loved ones, and many health issues including cancer. In 1978, through a compassionate, caring, nonjudgmental friend (who became my husband), I was introduced to his friend, Jesus.

Having learned so much about Jesus' love, forgiveness, faithfulness, and how he comforts us, there came a time when I questioned what to do with all of those struggles of life. Did they mean something? Did they happen for a reason?

After some much-needed Christian counseling, my answer came. God had comforted me through so many hard times, and it was time I shared that comfort with others.

Once I opened myself to the idea of comforting others, the question was "How?" God gave me the gift of singing, so I recorded a set of 48 songs with the focus on hope. Those songs have ministered and provided comfort to those who have depleted their energy by helping others, those who are grieving, families dealing with cancer, missionaries, hurricane victims, and so many others that have found themselves in hard times.

The music led to becoming a speaker, and both have led to writing a book. The music, speaking, and written words continue to be a comfort to many,

Blue Tassels

even though I would have never thought God would use my voice and pen to minister to others.

Maybe these ways of reaching out to comfort others are not your thing. Maybe it makes more sense for you to send a card, sit with someone for a while, offer a hug, or provide food or transportation.

We all have a story or two, and if you are reading this devotional, you will have more stories to come. Pray for God to show you where you can use the comfort he provided you to comfort others.

Have you gone through some tough situations in your life, and comfort has been provided? God comforts us in all our troubles **so that** we can comfort others.

Threads

Psalm 23:4; Psalm 119:76;
Romans 15:5; 1 Thessalonians 5:11

WEEK FIVE

TASSEL OF
RELATIONSHIP

Blue Tassels

DAY 1

Determined→Deliverance→Relationship

Mark 5:30-31 (NLT)

JESUS REALIZED AT ONCE that healing power had gone out from him, so he turned around in the crowd and asked, "Who touched my robe?"

His disciples said to him, "Look at this crowd pressing around you. How can you ask, 'Who touched me?'"

At the same moment the bleeding woman felt the bleeding stop and she knew she had been healed, Jesus felt the power leave his body. She touched the tassel, the bleeding vanished, and healing occurred.

Immediately, she felt and Jesus felt. His footsteps stopped. Disciples were questioning. The crowd was confused, and Jairus was frantic to get to his daughter. Jesus just stood still, the crowd still pressing forward, and the disciples trying to understand how he knew one particular person touched him.

The healed woman is still hidden among the crowd, most likely overwhelmed by emotion because of what just miraculously happened. She may have been fearful of having touched other people while trying to get to Jesus, or even making Jesus unclean. Was she aware that she interrupted his goal of getting to Jairus' dying daughter? Would the crowd hurl insults at her?

Her first inclination may have been to quietly slip away into the crowd. Jesus had other intentions. Healing the woman wasn't enough. He wanted a relationship with her; healing her heart, mind, and soul. She didn't make Jesus unclean. He made her clean.

We don't know exactly what Jesus looked like. I think of him with the children and how he blessed them and prayed for them. I believe he had eyes of compassion, arms of comfort, a voice of gentleness, and feet that have traveled many miles sharing the message of love and forgiveness. Children could feel his character.

My husband has a print of Richard Hook's "Head of Christ": the artist's idea of what Jesus looked like. For over 46 years I have looked at that picture and what stands out to me are his eyes: his eyes of compassion and love. There is something powerful about being able to look at Jesus, even though it's just someone's idea of his features, and knowing I have a relationship with this awesome person who was sent to earth and who ultimately died for me.

I believe Jesus wanted to look the woman in the eyes and let her know that he was offering so much more than physical healing.

Take time to develop your relationship with this man of compassion, comfort, and love. Read his word, pray to him, and get to know the one who died so you could spend eternity with him.

"Never is a woman more beautiful than when she looks in the face of her Savior and sees his love for her shining in his eyes."*

---

* Liz Curtis Higgs, *Embrace Grace* (Colorado Springs: WaterBrook Press, 2006), 46.

Threads

*Matthew 11:28-30; Matthew 19:13-15;
John 12:44-46*

Blue Tassels

DAY 2

Fixing Our Eyes on Jesus

Hebrews 12:1-3

THEREFORE, SINCE WE ARE surrounded by such a great cloud of witnesses, let us throw off everything that hinders and the sin that so easily entangles. And let us run with perseverance the race marked out for us, fixing our eyes on Jesus, the pioneer and perfecter of faith. For the joy set before him he endured the cross, scorning its shame, and sat down at the right hand of the throne of God. Consider him who endured such opposition from sinners, so that you will not grow weary and lose heart.

TASSEL OF RELATIONSHIP

I have a couple friends I can put in the category of that "great cloud of witnesses."

They were two special women who fought with everything they had, including fixing their eyes on Jesus: one with cancer persevering through treatments and one with long-term heart issues. To those of us on the outside, they seemed to never grow weary, though I'm sure there were moments when they did. Both loved and trusted and had faith in God and believed his promises.

As much as you tried to comfort them, they would turn around and be comforting to you. They continued to smile and carry on the best they could with daily living. Both stayed positive and yet were humbled by often asking for prayer. Do you have anyone you have known in your life who fits this category?

In Hebrews 11, we find a wonderful list of faith-filled people who lived in the past and never gave up running their race. They trusted, believed, and obeyed. Some were tortured and put into prison. They sacrificed and suffered. This great cloud of witnesses fixed their eyes on God.

God sent his son, Jesus, who endured the cross and died for them, and us, so we all can live together for all of eternity.

Nurture a relationship with Jesus. Fix your eyes on him. Believe. Trust. Obey. Have faith.

Threads

Psalm 105:1-4; Jeremiah 29:13

TASSEL OF RELATIONSHIP

DAY 3

Lord, I Want to See

Luke 18:35-43

As Jesus approached Jericho, a blind man was sitting by the roadside begging. When he heard the crowd going by, he asked what was happening. They told him, "Jesus of Nazareth is passing by."

He called out, "Jesus, Son of David, have mercy on me!"

Those who led the way rebuked him and told him to be quiet, but he shouted all the more, "Son of David, have mercy on me!"

Jesus stopped and ordered the man to be brought to him. When he came near, Jesus asked him, "What do you want me to do for you?"

"Lord, I want to see," he replied.

Jesus said to him, "Receive your sight; your faith has healed you." Immediately he received his sight and followed Jesus, praising God. When all the people saw it, they also praised God.

When he found out who was passing by, the blind man called out his name, "Jesus, Son of David!" He acknowledged Jesus as the Messiah. This showed he believed and had faith, even though he was blind.

The man was desperate to be able to see and determined to get the attention of Jesus, shouting out his name again after being rebuked by others. When the man said he wanted to see, Jesus immediately healed him.

The man became a praise-filled witness to Jesus' compassion and power and it led others to praise Jesus, too.

When I was in elementary school, each person in our class had to memorize a poem. The one I memorized was "Who Has Seen the Wind" by Christina Rossetti (1830-1894).

> Who has seen the wind?
> Neither I nor you.
> But when the leaves hang trembling,
> The wind is passing through.
> Who has seen the wind?
> Neither you nor I.
> But when the trees bow down their heads,
> The wind is passing by.
> *(Public Domain)*

I have often thought of this poem in connection with faith. Faith is the confidence that what we hope for will actually happen; it gives us assurance about things we cannot see. (Hebrews 11:1 ESV)

Have you ever believed in something you could not see? For instance, we cannot see the wind, but we know it is there because we can feel it and see the result of it blowing.

Jesus was no doubt face-to-face with the blind beggar, and yet without eye contact. The bleeding woman was probably behind Jesus in the crowd and crouching down so she could touch the hem of his robe, so their eyes didn't meet. When both were healed, their eyes met with Jesus'. The man's connection by sight was immediate; the woman's was after Jesus had her come forth.

Both had heard of Jesus and believed in his healing power. Both were determined and had faith they, too, would be healed. And the healing of both was just the start of their relationship with Jesus.

In our lives, circumstances happen and obstacles present themselves and it's hard to believe that God is still there because we are not seeing any answers to our pleas for help. We pray, we ask others for prayer, we read scripture, remain faithful, and believe he will answer.

The biggest step? We have reached out to him and have not given up. The Lord is faithful and hears our prayers.

Threads

*Psalm 27:14; Proverbs 3:5; Ecclesiastes 3:1;
1 Corinthians 16:13*

TASSEL OF RELATIONSHIP

DAY 4

The Good Shepherd

Psalm 23

THE LORD IS MY shepherd, I lack nothing.

He makes me lie down in green pastures, he leads me beside quiet waters, he refreshes my soul.

He guides me along the right paths for his name's sake.

Even though I walk through the darkest valley, I will fear no evil, for you are with me; your rod and your staff, they comfort me.

You prepare a table before me in the presence of my enemies. You anoint my head with oil; my cup overflows.

Surely your goodness and love will follow me all the days of my life, and I will dwell in the house of the Lord forever.

Blue Tassels

David was a harpist, a singer, a writer, a shepherd, and a king. One of the songs he wrote from his experience of being a shepherd was Psalm 23. With his experience, he understood the relationship between a shepherd and his sheep.

Shepherds protect their flock from danger, see that their needs are met in rest and food, and using a staff, they guide them on their paths. Oil is poured on them to protect the ears and nose from insects, and to soothe the scrapes and scratches they receive walking through fields on rough ground.

The relationship between the Lord as our shepherd and us is similar. He provides rest and refreshment, direction in our daily lives, comfort through hard seasons, and in times of fear, protection.

As with the woman in our story, and so many other stories in the scriptures, our shepherd gives healing, love, mercy, and the hope of eternal life. He is faithful, good, a rescuer and protector, and is loyal. He is righteous, patient, gentle, and kind. He is truth.

Follow this Shepherd daily. He will be your sure-footed guide.

Threads

*Psalm 100; Ezekiel 34:31; Matthew 9:36;
Luke 19:10; John 10:11*

Blue Tassels

DAY 5

Sharing the Tassel of Relationship

Psalm 34:4-5

I SOUGHT THE LORD, and he answered me; he delivered me from all my fears. Those who look to him are radiant; their faces are never covered with shame.

TASSEL OF RELATIONSHIP

Have you ever walked in a garden that has seen harsh weather and needs watering?

Just like a garden, there are times when we seem "dry". The dry conditions may come through pain (caused by circumstances beyond our control, wrong choices of others, or our own wrong choices).

Seek help, if needed. Share your struggles with a trustworthy friend so they can pray for you. Find your struggle in a promise book and read the recommended scriptures. Pray. He is listening.

When we allow God to "water us," and fill us with virtues in the image of his son, our hearts become radiant. They are filled with love, joy, peace, patience, kindness, goodness, faithfulness, gentleness, and self-control (Galatians 5:22-23).

Once our hearts are filled, our attitudes can change, which changes our behaviors. We learn to forgive. We both feel and extend compassion. We take steps to strengthen our faith. We develop a hunger to hear God through prayer and scripture reading. Through worship, our radiant hearts shine through our faces, and people can, figuratively, see the glory of God because of us.

Hearts→attitudes→behaviors→faces→sharing Jesus Christ. God changes the way the outside looks by changing us inside . . . and we reflect him.

Return to radiance and reflect the relationship you have with your Lord. The longer you spend in the garden with him, the more you will see him

Blue Tassels

love, care, and water you. Others will notice the radiant bouquet and ask where you got it. Share your beautiful flowers!

"Where the grace of God is missed, bitterness is born. But where the grace of God is embraced, forgiveness flourishes. . . . The longer we walk in the garden, the more likely we are to smell like flowers. The more we immerse ourselves in grace, the more likely we are to give grace."*

* Max Lucado, *In The Grip of Grace* (Dallas: Word Publishing, 1996), 154.

Threads

*Psalm 63:1; Proverbs 27:19; Isaiah 58:11;
Hosea 10:12; Philippians 2:1-4*

WEEK SIX

TASSEL OF LOVE

Blue Tassels

DAY 1

Determined→Deliverance→Love

Mark 5:32 (NLT)

BUT HE KEPT ON looking around to see who had done it.

Jesus had already asked who touched his robe. His disciples were anxious because of the pressing crowds, but Jesus wanted to see who touched him. Jesus kept looking, basically ignoring his disciples and all of the curious people on the crowded street.

He may have known who she was, where she was from, and what the malady was he healed, but he wanted her to take the first step of acknowledgment. He would be able to see her face to face, radiating his love, compassion, and comfort. She, in turn, would physically show the faith she had in his ability to heal, all while the followers stood listening and watching. They witnessed how Jesus felt the flow of power and showed compassion by wanting to see the person on the receiving end.

In the busyness of the moment, the frustration of the disciples, and what must have felt like an endless interruption for Jairus, Jesus was patient. He was patient with that personal contact, and her making herself known.

When she saw Jesus, who took away her horrible long-term sickness, she would know that regardless of her circumstances of being sick, unclean, rejected, and all the emotions tied up with her condition, she would only see his unconditional love.

Jesus, in his patience, looks for you. Your circumstances do not matter. Your struggles with life and feelings of hopelessness do not matter. Your doubts and unconfessed sin do not matter.

Blue Tassels

You can be in the very middle of experiencing the driest season of your life, and Jesus is looking for you and wanting you to respond, showing your face to him. Reach out to him. He loves you.

Threads

Psalm 86:15; Psalm 136; Ephesians 3:16-19

Blue Tassels

DAY 2

Sensing the Savior

2 Corinthians 2:14-15

BUT THANKS BE TO God, who always leads us as captives in Christ's triumphal procession and uses us to spread the aroma of the knowledge of him everywhere. For we are to God the pleasing aroma of Christ among those who are being saved and those who are perishing.

Many weeks (sometimes months) before actual holidays (e.g., New Year's, Easter, Fourth of July, Thanksgiving, and Christmas), we see the stores explode with noise makers, paper plates, jelly beans, spring décor, fireworks, sales on everything barbecue, flags, themed food platters, turkey decorations, ornaments, lights, hustle and bustle of shoppers, and so much more sensory overload.

We smell the cooking of holiday dinners and the celebratory foods. We taste the results of all the preparations. We hear everything from Christmas noels to Easter praises and the national anthem to songs of thanksgiving. And we feel hugs from friends and family.

I'm sure Jesus experienced sensory overload, because of the times he drew away to quiet places to be by himself.

Think of what he experienced the day he healed the bleeding woman: the smells of the markets they passed and the crowd pressing against him, the sights of stone buildings and narrow streets filled with people watching and wondering, the chatter and pleas of those who were reaching out wanting healing and more teaching.

Why was there a crowd? Were they there just to see this man so many had talked about? Were they hoping to hear more messages? Did he have an "aroma" about him that drew the crowds?

What was this aroma that, as believers, we are called to spread? A partial list of these characteristics of Christ . . . these pleasing aromas . . . would include his compassion, love, forgiveness, kindness, patience, and humility.

Pray to have the aroma of Christ. Taste by feeding on his Word. See the stars on a clear night and follow him. Reach out and touch the hem of his robe, breathe in his breath of life, and be still to hear his message.

The next time you are with family or friends, at your job, shopping, or eating out at a restaurant, share his pleasing aroma. Someone who never knew Jesus may sense the Savior through you.

Threads

1 Corinthians 13:4-8a; Ephesians 5:1-2

DAY 3

Love Language

John 3:16; Romans 5:6-8

For God so loved the world that he gave his one and only Son, that whoever believes in him shall not perish but have eternal life.

You see, at just the right time, when we were still powerless, Christ died for the ungodly. Very rarely will anyone die for a righteous person, though for a good person someone might possibly dare to die. But God demonstrates his own love for us in this: While we were still sinners, Christ died for us.

Growing up in Indiana, I traveled with family in the summer to Wyoming where my grandparents lived. The real excitement hit when we crossed the Mississippi River, which indicated we were on our way west.

When I think of those trips, I remember looking so forward to the days of unconditional love from Grandpa and Grandma. When we arrived, there would be kisses from Grandpa, with his stubbly chin scratching against my cheek.

The smells in the house were heavenly: Grandma had been baking all of our favorites to have for the week. When we traveled to their cabin in the Big Horn Mountains, Grandma made pancakes on her large griddle and Grandpa took us fishing. Their love language toward us was time, hugs, and food.

Love language expressed here on earth doesn't come close to the sacrificial love demonstrated by Jesus. Matthew (27:55) and Mark (15:41) record that many women were present at the crucifixion. I wonder if the woman who had been healed in our story was there. I wonder how many who were in the crowd had been directly impacted by Jesus and his love.

There are times in our lives when we have felt unloved. People have failed us and have spoken harsh words against us. Maybe family life growing up was not as loving as it should have been. As a result, we have had a hard time showing love.

Maybe you have reached out in love, only to have it rejected. One of the hardest lessons I have learned is how to love a person even if the love is not returned.

What is your love language? If Jesus had a love language, maybe it was experiencing the faith that people showed by following him. In talking with his disciples, Jesus says, "Love one another. As I have loved you, so you must love one another. By this, everyone will know that you are my disciples if you love one another." (John 13:34-35)

"Your love, Lord, reaches to the heavens, your faithfulness to the skies. How priceless is your unfailing love, O God! People take refuge in the shadow of your wings." (Psalm 36:5,7)

Take refuge under his wings.

"Joy, peace and stability come from believing that every circumstance that touches our lives has first been filtered through His fingers of love and is part of a great, eternal plan that He is working out in this world and in our lives." (Nancy Leigh Moss)

Threads

Isaiah 54:10; Luke 6:27-31

DAY 4

Inner Strength

Ephesians 3:16-19 (NLT)

I PRAY THAT FROM his glorious, unlimited resources he will empower you with inner strength through his Spirit. Then Christ will make his home in your hearts as you trust in him. Your roots will grow down into God's love and keep you strong. And may you have the power to understand, as all God's people should, how wide, how long, how high, and how deep his love is. May you experience the love of Christ, though it is too great to understand fully. Then you will be made complete with all the fullness of life and power that comes from God.

For over 24 years I worked as a paraprofessional in a program for disabled young adults. Once on a community outing, we were learning to use the light rail. I was sitting in a handicapped area facing the aisle, and on the other side were two rows of seats.

In the front seat, I noticed a woman lying across the seat. She was dressed in many layers, with a hat and covering for her head. Beside her were a couple of large bags filled with possessions. It seemed obvious she was homeless.

At one point, the train car jostled a little and her head covering fell off. She was struggling to get it back on her head when I noticed most of her hair had fallen out. Then I noticed a hospital band on her wrist. Did she have cancer? Was she having chemo?

My heart was instantly stirred by the Holy Spirit telling me to let her know that she was beautiful and God loved her. My body began shaking, knowing I needed to obey.

When we reached our stop, I crossed the aisle, lightly touched her shoulder, and told her she was beautiful and that God loved her. She flinched and moaned. In the seat behind her was an elderly couple. I noticed the man just shook his head, but the woman beside him looked right at me, smiled, and nodded. She understood the love of God.

When we have the Holy Spirit and our roots are deep in Christ, enabling us to understand his love, we will be given the inner strength needed to share that powerful love.

Did the woman know of God's love? I hope somehow that day, she did. What about the lady sitting behind her? I believe her nodding head and winsome smile told me she understood the deep love of God.

And what do I do with all of the love inside of me? Proclaim good news to others!

I love the imagery of how roots will grow down into God's love and keep us strong. It reminds me of Isaiah 61:1-3 . . . proclaiming good news to the poor, binding up the brokenhearted, proclaiming freedom for the captives and release from darkness for the prisoners . . . to comfort all who mourn, provide for those who grieve—to bestow on them beauty, joy, a garment of praise—and they will be called oaks of righteousness, a planting of the Lord for the display of his splendor.

Threads

Psalm 89:1-2; 1 Peter 4:10-11

DAY 5

Sharing the Tassel of Love

Romans 12:9-16 (NLT)

DON'T JUST PRETEND TO love others. Really love them. Hate what is wrong. Hold tightly to what is good. Love each other with genuine affection, and take delight in honoring each other. Never be lazy, but work hard and serve the Lord enthusiastically. Rejoice in our confident hope. Be patient in trouble, and keep on praying. When God's people are in need, be ready to help them. Always be eager to practice hospitality.

Bless those who persecute you. Don't curse them; pray that God will bless them. Be happy with those who are happy, and weep with those who weep. Live in harmony with each other. Don't be too proud to enjoy the company of ordinary people. And don't think you know it all!

TASSEL OF LOVE

When my son was somewhere in the toddler stage, he said to a teenager at church, "Don't worry, be happy." Even at that innocent age, he was trying to encourage someone who appeared sad to him. Was that showing love? Sure!

Those who attended a church camp or were involved in youth groups may remember a song that was usually sung in a round, "Love, love, love, love. The gospel in a word is love. Love thy neighbor as thy brother. Love, love, love." (Public Domain)

Loving someone sounds easy, but what about a friend who follows another crowd and rejects you? How about the family member who abandons you? Maybe it is that homeless person begging on the side of the road. It could be a rude coworker or an upset store clerk who just got chewed out by a customer. They are all our neighbors.

God loves you with an unfailing love.

Love God, love yourself, and love others. Continue to praise God, pray for your needs, and pray for your neighbors. Then remember to thank God for his love and provisions in your life. Thank him for the neighbors he brings to your attention.

Threads

Luke 10:25-27; John 13:34-35; John 15:9-21

WEEK SEVEN

TASSEL OF FORGIVENESS

DAY 1

Delivered→Forgiveness

Mark 5:33 (NLT)

THEN THE FRIGHTENED WOMAN, trembling at the realization of what had happened to her, came and fell to her knees in front of him and told him what she had done.

TASSEL OF FORGIVENESS

Have you ever experienced so much fear that your knees were knocking together?

When getting in trouble as a young child, I remember the fear of having done something I shouldn't have done, and, back in those days, getting a spanking. As a teenager, well, I was getting in trouble all the time and the fear was of getting grounded . . . again.

As an adult, fear was having my first child and leaving the hospital to head home with this new human being, who was so small and totally dependent on my husband and me.

I was afraid when I got up in front of a congregation and sang a special song. (That was the knocking knees for me!) Later on in life, I made a big mistake and, in fear, needed to confess, repent, and ask forgiveness.

I believe the woman in our story was terrified of confessing she had broken laws surrounding being unclean and pushing her way through a crowd of "clean." Had she blamed herself for somehow causing the bleeding for twelve years?

I am sure during those long years, she felt anger with how she was treated. Her family had deserted her and friends were nowhere to be found. When people noticed her, she was criticized and hated for being in public while unclean.

And yet, here was this man, Jesus, who had eyes of compassion, a voice of understanding, and an attitude of love, who had healed her horrible affliction. He knew she had taken a chance, as an unclean woman, to be in the crowded streets and try to touch his robe. When she fell to her knees, her posture showed respect, humility, and possibly an apology for having touched his robe.

I'm not sure she anticipated the forgiveness that followed.

Fearful and trembling, she shared her story. Though the crowd was still present, when she looked into his eyes, I imagine Jesus was the only person she saw or heard at that moment. All other faces on the busy street were blurred and the surrounding noise was silenced. All she saw in front of her was his love and compassion that healed her body and touched her soul.

Do we not know and understand how God could forgive us for our sins? Are we sorry for waiting so long to seek him; to acknowledge we are helpless without him?

He is in front of us waiting for us to reach out to him, to look into his eyes, and share our stories with him.

Threads

Psalm 9:9-11; Psalm 19:14; Psalm 130

Blue Tassels

DAY 2

Freedom Within

Psalm 146:5-8

BLESSED ARE THOSE WHOSE help is the God of Jacob, whose hope is in the Lord their God.

He is the Maker of heaven and earth, the sea, and everything in them—he remains faithful forever.

He upholds the cause of the oppressed and gives food to the hungry.

The Lord sets prisoners free, the Lord gives sight to the blind, the Lord lifts up those who are bowed down, the Lord loves the righteous.

From 2012 through 2016 I had the opportunity to minister through word and song to some beautiful women at Shakopee Women's Prison here in Minnesota. Never hearing their specific stories, I knew these women represented offenses from murder to dealing drugs, from stealing to other major and minor offenses.

There was one inmate I had the experience of offering encouragement and hope to who was very prominent in the local news. During four visits to the prison, I witnessed her expressions of deep sorrow, while sitting in the middle of the group, gradually change until she was singing worship songs and smiling in the second row.

The difference in the weeks? According to a short conversation we had the last time I saw her, I believe she had grown to love the Lord and through prayers and the repentance of her crime, God granted her freedom within. He lifted her head once again.

Even though these women would love the freedom outside the walls, they could feel freedom in Christ within the walls. There is no doubt some dealt with remorse, stress, sickness, anger, loneliness, and all types of physical and emotional pain, but when they reached out in prayer, asking for forgiveness, finding that relationship with Jesus Christ and trusting him . . . he was faithful "to proclaim freedom for the prisoners." (Luke 4:18)

In Mark 5:29 we read that "Immediately the bleeding stopped and [the woman] could feel in her body that she had been healed of her terrible condition." We know her physical ailment was healed. Knowing how physical sickness can affect our emotional state, no doubt her stress, anger, and feelings of rejection were healed in time as well. She had freedom within.

Have faith in God and surrender your life to him; maybe for the first time or maybe for the twenty-first time. You, too, can be given that freedom within.

Threads

Romans 8:1-4; Ephesians 4:29-32; 1 John 1:9

Blue Tassels

DAY 3

A Slice of Humble Pie

1 Peter 5:5-7, 10

. . . YOU who are younger, submit yourselves to your elders. All of you, clothe yourselves with humility toward one another, because, "God opposes the proud but shows favor to the humble."

Humble yourselves, therefore, under God's mighty hand, that he may lift you up in due time. Cast all your anxiety on him because he cares for you.

And the God of all grace, who called you to his eternal glory in Christ, after you have suffered a little while, will himself restore you and make you strong, firm and steadfast.

Let's make Crumble Apple Pie, one of my family's favorites!

We begin with the crust. The crust is needed to hold the pie together and aid in scooping a piece out of the pan. Then we mix sliced apples, lemon juice, sugar, flour, and cinnamon to create the filling, which is then poured into the pie base.

Preferring a crumble topping over a pastry topping, we mix flour, seasonings, and butter and sprinkle the mixture on top of the apples. After baking, serve warm, possibly with a dollop of ice cream.

Let's compare the crust of the pie to the base, the foundation, of a life in Christ. In a nutshell (or a pie shell), what's it all about? "[God] has shown you, O mortal, what is good. And what does the Lord require of you? To act justly and to love mercy and to walk humbly with your God." (Micah 6:8)

Next we have the filling, the truth of God that fills the scriptures.

"In your relationships with one another, have the same mindset as Christ Jesus: who, being in very nature God, did not consider equality with God something to be used to his own advantage; rather, he made himself nothing by taking the very nature of a servant, being made in human likeness. And being found in appearance as a man, he humbled himself by becoming obedient to death—even death on a cross!" (Philippians 2:5-11)

And now, the topping of our apple pie, which is the part that is seen. This represents the part of our lives, our humility, that others see. "Therefore if you have any encouragement from being united with Christ, if any comfort from his love, if any common sharing in the Spirit, if any tenderness and compassion, then make my joy complete by being like-minded, having the same love, being one in spirit and of one mind. Do nothing out of selfish ambition or vain conceit. Rather, in humility value others above yourselves, not looking to your own interests but each of you to the interests of the others." (Philippians 2:1-4)

Do we need to add a delicious scoop of ice cream? This tops our pie with the sweetness of God's promises. "God opposes the proud but shows favor to the humble. Humble yourselves, therefore, under God's mighty hand, that he may lift you up in due time. Cast all your anxiety on him because he cares for you." (1 Peter 5:5-7)

When the woman realized what happened to her, she fell to her knees before Jesus. Trembling in fear, she dropped to a humble position. Her faith took her to Jesus' robe; his healing took her to her knees.

She surrendered all her being to Jesus. Most likely, not even realizing it, her humility in the face of the Lord's healing and forgiveness was an example to the crowd surrounding them.

Humble yourself, cast your anxieties on the Lord, and be restored. Others will notice.

Threads

*Psalm 24:4-10; James 2:5-11;
James 3:17; James 4:10*

DAY 4

Forgiveness

1 John 1:5-9

THIS IS THE MESSAGE we have heard from him and declare to you: God is light; in him there is no darkness at all. If we claim to have fellowship with him and yet walk in the darkness, we lie and do not live out the truth. But if we walk in the light, as he is in the light, we have fellowship with one another, and the blood of Jesus, his Son, purifies us from all sin.

If we claim to be without sin, we deceive ourselves and the truth is not in us. If we confess our sins, he is faithful and just and will forgive us our sins and purify us from all unrighteousness.

In 1978, feeling torn down, used up, and worthless, I realized something needed to change. It was then I met a wonderful Christian man who led me to Jesus.

On May 25, 1978, I asked for forgiveness, confessed Jesus as Lord, was baptized in his name, and began a new life in him. Washed "white as snow" (Isaiah 1:18), I now had the hope of eternal life. Jesus continues to love me unconditionally, demonstrate compassion, and provide comfort and peace.

Through my walk with the Lord, he has taught me I needed to forgive others as I was forgiven.

I had been abused physically and emotionally, betrayed, and abandoned. How could I say "That's okay" to those people?

However, I learned that forgiveness is not condoning the offender's actions. It is not saying, "That's okay." Instead, it puts the situation in God's hands and allows you to move forward, healed from the emotional scars created by others.

The hardest person to forgive . . . is ourselves. We tend to ask the question, "Why? Why does temptation have such a firm grip?" We tend to be overcome by guilt and shame, asking ourselves if it was our fault we were in certain situations. "What was I thinking?"

God wants us to feel loved, be full of joy, experience peace, and have hope.

TASSEL OF FORGIVENESS

Ask God for forgiveness, accepting him into your life. Forgive anyone who has caused you pain. Forgive yourself. Forgiveness is trusting God. Forgiveness is surrendering. Forgiveness is freeing ourselves to heal.

Blue Tassels

Threads

Mark 11:25; John 14:6; Philippians 1:6

TASSEL OF FORGIVENESS

DAY 5

Sharing the Tassel of Forgiveness

Colossians 3:12-14

THEREFORE, AS GOD'S CHOSEN people, holy and dearly loved, clothe yourselves with compassion, kindness, humility, gentleness and patience. Bear with each other and forgive one another if any of you has a grievance against someone. Forgive as the Lord forgave you. And over all these virtues put on love, which binds them all together in perfect unity.

Have you ever looked at your closet full of clothes and still not had a thing to wear?

Are they too small or too big? Just not in style for the current fads? Maybe they're not the right color for the special event?

Boutiques seem to be the trend for fashion-forward clothing. They offer themes such as, "Bring Sunshine to Your Closet," "We provide a personalized shopping experience," and "Be Transformed into a Princess!"

How about we shop at God's Virtue Boutique?

First, we need to clean out the old "clothes," such as selfishness, malice, inappropriate pride, disrespect, anxiety, bitterness, worldly passion, greed, and hate. God's Virtue Boutique includes "clothes" of compassion, kindness, humility, gentleness, peace, patience, forgiveness, self-control, thankfulness, and love.

Do clothes really "make" the person? These kinds of clothes sure do. Surrendering our lives to God causes wonderful changes.

When we have emptied ourselves, God begins to dress us with the virtues he intended, in the image of his son, Jesus. We are clothed in forgiveness for others as Christ forgave us. When the inside changes, the outside follows.

Magnifying the Lord in our daily lives can lead to changing the lives of others. They may want to clean out their closet and head to God's Virtue Boutique.

Threads

Proverbs 31:25; Romans 13:14; 2 Corinthians 4:6

WEEK EIGHT

TASSEL OF REST

Blue Tassels

DAY 1

Deliverance→Rest

Mark 5:34 (NLT)

AND HE SAID TO her, "Daughter, your faith has made you well. Go in peace. Your suffering is over."

TASSEL OF REST

Jesus leaves one crowd, gets in a boat with the disciples, and embarks on the short journey across the water to Capernaum. Yes, another crowd waiting.

The crowds usually included his closest friends and faithful followers, those who sought healing, a few who were curious, and those who criticized. This walk down the street was no different.

Then, desperate pleas are heard from Jairus, the leader of a local synagogue, for Jesus to touch and heal his dying daughter. Jesus continues with him when he is stopped by a sudden feeling of energy leaving his body. He asks who touched his robe. Everyone stops and looks around. The talking subsides and sandals shuffle in the dirt. When no answer comes, he keeps looking.

This desperate, weak, and weary woman found Jesus surrounded by a group of people. She was determined to make her way through the crowd to touch his robe, believing that she would be healed.

Immediately upon touching the hem of Jesus' robe, her body responded and she knew Jesus had healed her ailment. She knew Jesus wanted to know who touched him, and in spite of her fear, she spoke up and shared her whole story.

At this point of deliverance, did Jesus kneel to her level, or did she stand to be at his level? Either way, his eyes met hers. What did he see? Faith. What did she see? Jesus' compassion, mercy, and love.

His first word was "Daughter . . ." This was a term of endearment she had not heard in 12 long years. Perhaps shedding a few tears and breathing a sigh of relief, she realized her desperation was over. With a crowd of quiet onlookers leaning in to hear the words of Jesus, she experiences his unconditional love.

There is no mention of Jesus criticizing her for being unclean. Nor does he berate her for having interrupted the trip to Jairus' house.

"Your faith has made you well." Her body could rest now. No more bleeding. Her faith in Jesus is what healed her. There was no power of healing in the clothes or the tassel. She was delivered because of her faith, her belief in Jesus, and that he could heal. Not because of the touch of the robe.

Threads

Colossians 2:6; Hebrews 11:1

Blue Tassels

DAY 2

A Beautiful Mess

Matthew 11:28-30 (NLT)

THEN JESUS SAID, "COME to me, all of you who are weary and carry heavy burdens, and I will give you rest. Take my yoke upon you. Let me teach you, because I am humble and gentle at heart, and you will find rest for your souls. For my yoke is easy to bear, and the burden I give you is light."

Some days we feel we are a beautiful mess. There are so many "issues in my tissues".

Love has been compromised, joy has been hard to find, and peace and patience struggle within. Kindness, goodness, and faithfulness? They are inside me somewhere, but the messiness of life has hidden them from view. Gentleness and self-control have become difficult.

Have you ever longed for any of these virtues? All of these virtues? What we look like on the outside when these issues are inside is not very attractive.

Take a moment and insert your name throughout the scripture for today, for example, "Come to me, Debbie, you are weary . . . "

How can we stir the smoldering embers of the good inside us and see it burst into flame?

When Jesus struggled with being overwhelmed by the crowds—people asking, pleading, and criticizing—he would take some time to rest. Where could we find Jesus resting? Walking beside the sea, on a mountainside, on the water sleeping in a boat, or in a garden in prayer with his Father.

Where can you find rest for your mind, body, and soul? Find places where you can pray, journal your feelings, listen to music, be still in silence, and listen to God's voice.

Some of us find rest in looking outside of our "issues" and taking time to serve others. We can "ignite others" by offering a listening ear, sending a greeting card, making a phone call, donating clothing, or providing a basket of food or favorite things. Do you know anyone who could benefit from a Bible, a promise book, encouraging inspirational music, or a prayer shawl?

Are you a beautiful mess? Jesus loves you and thinks you are beautiful! In his gentleness, he takes on our mess and provides quiet waters where we can be refreshed and find rest for our souls. Seek him and the tranquility he provides.

Threads

*Psalm 46; Psalm 139:14; Proverbs 11:25;
Romans 3:23-25; Colossians 3:15-17*

Blue Tassels

DAY 3

A Place of Rest

Psalm 23:1-3

THE LORD IS MY shepherd, I lack nothing. He makes me lie down in green pastures, he leads me beside quiet waters, he refreshes my soul. He guides me along the right paths for his name's sake.

TASSEL OF REST

Our scripture is a psalm written by David, a shepherd. He knew the feeling of laying down in a pasture and the rest it provided.

I can see him reaching a place of quiet waters for the sheep to drink and for him to splash the refreshing water on his face. As a shepherd, he would know the countryside and the paths for the sheep to follow. Being a shepherd was hard work, and I am sure those times of rest were precious moments when he could relax, refresh, and refocus.

Many weekends when I was growing up, my family would go camping by a lake. As an adult, I now understand why we camped so often. It was a place of rest for my full-time working parents. These were days of relaxing, having fun, and enjoying family time.

When I was in high school, the camping ceased, but we still made time to go skiing, usually choosing times in the morning when we knew the lake was least crowded. We also looked for carved-out areas of the lakes where the water seemed the most calm. When I think of rest, I remember those times skiing on the glassy surface. So smooth, no worries about rough waters . . . peaceful, happy times.

The woman Jesus healed probably didn't have much rest. Where did she live and in what kind of humble structure did she stay? Because of the weakness and fatigue that came with her disease, she probably slept a lot, but I am sure it wasn't truly a restful sleep.

During the day, she exhausted all her resources in her search for healing. She avoided people because of being unclean, but still needed to take care of basic needs like food and cleanliness, all while dealing with quiet ridicule and loud judgment.

When Jesus said, "Your faith has made you well," the rest from physical and emotional exhaustion must have been an amazing feeling. And then to realize that not only her body was healed, but her soul as well? How calming, and yet exhilarating, that must have felt!

To sleep is one thing, but to have a definite time of rest and refreshment, to be able to refocus and experience peace within our souls, is another.

Beginning today, find that place and time to pray. Pray for a relaxing rest. Pray for refreshment and for your mind to be refocused. Pray for God to heal you physically and emotionally. He will provide you with pastures of rest, quiet waters to refresh, and paths of righteousness.

Threads

Psalm 95:6-7; Proverbs 4:18; Jeremiah 31:25-26

Blue Tassels

DAY 4

Beauty in the Singer

Zephaniah 3:17 (NLT)

For the Lord your God is living among you. He is a mighty savior. He will take delight in you with gladness. With his love, he will calm all your fears. He will rejoice over you with joyful songs.

Music and singing, in some form or another, are mentioned numerous times throughout scripture.

A descendant of Adam and Eve named Jubal, played the harp and flute (Genesis 4:21). The first and last songs of the Bible were songs from God's servant, Moses: From the song of deliverance when Moses and the people praised the Lord (Exodus 15), to the last song recorded in scripture found in Revelation 15.

Music was played on wind, string, and percussion instruments. Song themes included songs of lament, narration, thankfulness, praise, and worship. Though there are many other poems and songs in the scriptures, the book of Psalms includes 150 songs, poems, and prayers from different years in Israel's history.

I love visiting nursing care facilities and singing to the clients. The expressions on the residents' faces when hymns are sung are priceless.

My mother suffered from dementia, which, unfortunately, only enhanced the mean spirit she demonstrated most of my life. But when I visited her in the nursing home, she always wanted me to play piano and sing. Though my piano playing was definitely not professional, I could sing. Others would gather in the front room of the home and I could feel the sense of calm arise when they joined in singing the hymns. Even mostly nonverbal residents would move their mouths, remembering the hymns of old.

For a short time, their faces reflected comfort, peace, and rest. Music soothed their souls.

Music covers the entire earth with a power that can soothe like a lullaby or ramp up our joyful excitement. Music can celebrate those who are alive and remember those who are not. Lyrics can express love, joy, personal stories, journeys in life, loss, hope, and rest.

"Where words fail, music speaks." (Hans Christian Andersen)

"Let the message of Christ dwell among you richly as you teach and admonish one another with all wisdom through psalms, hymns, and songs from the Spirit, singing to God with gratitude in your hearts." (Colossians 3:16)

Is today like any other? How is your mind, body, and spirit? Listen to some inspirational, encouraging music. Allow the message to dwell in you richly and provide you with rest for your soul. Rest in the knowledge that God rejoices over you with singing.

TASSEL OF REST

Threads
Genesis 4:41; Exodus 15:1-21; Psalm 5:11; Psalm 68:4; Psalm 95:1-2; Psalm 104:33; Revelation 15:3-4

Blue Tassels

DAY 5

Sharing the Tassel of Rest

Matthew 5:14-16

YOU ARE THE LIGHT of the world. A town built on a hill cannot be hidden. Neither do people light a lamp and put it under a bowl. Instead they put it on its stand, and it gives light to everyone in the house. In the same way, let your light shine before others, that they may see your good deeds and glorify your Father in heaven.

Being open and honest here: I was struggling with today's devotion, realizing the scripture I was going to use was a repeat and most of what I wanted to say I had said in the rest of this week's devotions. (Sometimes, writers struggle . . . gasp!)

In looking for rest myself, I prayed, searched scriptures, and did more research. God landed me in Matthew 5. Yes! One of the best ways to share rest is to show rest. The same is true for all of God's virtues that we receive from him.

I also turned to a bit of modern technology with Bing's AI writing app, Copilot. I typed "helping others find rest." This poem is what it produced:

Rest, *a gentle harbor for weary souls, where burdens find solace and worries cease*
In its quiet embrace, hearts mend and console, a refuge of peace, a sanctuary of release.
Guiding others to rest, *a noble endeavor, like a lighthouse beacon on stormy seas*
We extend our hands, hearts open, forever those who seek solace, yearning for ease.
In the hush of twilight, *when shadows fall, we offer respite, a haven from life's strife*
A kind word, a warm smile, a listening ear, helping weary wanderers find rest in life.
So let us be beacons, *spreading compassion wide Guiding souls toward rest, side by side.*
For in lifting others, we find our own reprieve And the world becomes a gentler place to live.

Therefore, be that lighthouse, guiding others toward Christ and the rest he offers.

We can extend our hands, offer open hearts, and have a kind word, a warm smile, and a listening ear. All the while, show them how you experience Jesus Christ as your refuge, your helper in times of need, your comforter, your redeemer, and lead them to times of rest in him.

The woman in our story knew that if she touched the robe of Jesus, she would be healed. She heard that truth from others. Faith had made her well and her life was forever changed in Christ.

Threads

*Exodus 31:17; Psalm 91:1; John 14:6; Hebrews 4:9-11;
1 Peter 5:10, 1 John 3:19-24*

WEEK NINE

TASSEL OF PEACE

Blue Tassels

DAY 1

Delivered→Peace

Mark 5:34 (NLT)

AND HE SAID TO her, "Daughter, your faith has made you well. Go in peace. Your suffering is over."

TASSEL OF PEACE

It took me a few moments to think of times of peace in my life. I needed to sit back, breathe, and pray for God to show me those times.

Laying out in the open grass at night and looking at the stars . . . Yes, that was peaceful. After giving birth, when each of my four babies were laid on my chest. Peace.

I've been through 21 major surgeries, each of which had risks of their own. But the one I didn't have peace about was my heart ablation. Other surgeries were just fixing or replacing a bone or a torn muscle, but this was my heart, an organ that I can't live without! When I woke up from surgery and realized everything was going to be fine, there was definitely a feeling of peace.

None of my experiences can compare to the 12-year long experience this woman had endured.

All she wanted was to be healed of her horrible, long-term physical issue. She had given so much to try to fix her failing physical body: because she was "unclean", she lost relationships, which led to loneliness, and her financial resources were depleted.

Somewhere she had heard stories of this healing man, Jesus. From desperation to determination, she made a plan. A plan to just touch his robe, thinking if she touched any part of his body, she would make him unclean.

That determination led to action, action led to touching, and touching led to healing. What I don't believe she expected was the other gifts that came from the healer.

Not only had she received healing, but also the endearing name of Daughter. She received rest for her body and freedom for all the areas of her life her sickness had affected. And don't forget peace. "Go in peace," Jesus said. Those gifts revealed his love, compassion, and power.

How I wish we knew the rest of the story, but we do know this. Her faith healed her, leading to rest, freedom from her sickness, and peace. No more bleeding, and her strength was restored. No more criticism of being unclean in public. Family and friends would accept her in their circle again. Peaceful sleep. Peace knowing that Jesus was her Lord and Savior.

Threads

*Isaiah 9:6; Jeremiah 29:11-14;
2 Thessalonians 3:16*

DAY 2

Woman at the Well: Cherished, Caught, Comforted

John 4:13-15, 25-26, 28-30, 40-42 (NLT)

JESUS REPLIED, "ANYONE WHO drinks this water will soon become thirsty again. But those who drink the water I give will never be thirsty again. It becomes a fresh, bubbling spring within them, giving them eternal life." "Please, sir," the woman said, "give me this water! Then I'll never be thirsty again, and I won't have to come here to get water."

The woman said, "I know the Messiah is coming—the one who is called Christ. When he comes, he will explain everything to us."

The woman left her water jar beside the well and ran back to the village, telling everyone, "Come and see a man who told me everything I ever did! Could he possibly be the Messiah?" So the people came streaming from the village to see him.

When they came out to see him, they begged him to stay in their village. So he stayed for two days, long enough for many more to hear his message and believe.

Then they said to the woman, "Now we believe, not just because of what you told us, but because we have heard him ourselves. Now we know that he is indeed the Savior of the world." (Read the entire story in the *Threads* section.)

"This is a reminder today that you aren't defined by what you've done, what you've experienced, how you felt, or even what others say about you. Only the person who gave you life has the right to define you. You are exactly who God says you are. You are chosen. You are loved, You're a daughter of the King. You are radiant." (Priscilla Shirer)

The Samaritan woman's King cherished, caught, and comforted her.

Cherished her enough to stop at the well, spend time talking with her, and explain how he wanted true followers who would worship him in spirit and truth.

Caught her in her time of being an outcast because of her messy life, explaining to her how he could help and heal through his living water.

She was **Comforted** in his presence, his words, and his love that hit the deepest part of her heart.

Out of the excitement and peace of his presence, words, and love, she turned her misery into ministry by telling the others in her town about Jesus. Then those people experienced being cherished, caught, and comforted; receiving his peace into their lives as well.

Have you felt cherished? Has Jesus caught you and comforted you? If not, seek him with all your heart. There will be no regret.

If you have, your excitement should be shared with others who may not know a King is waiting for them. A King who cherishes them, will catch them from their pain, and provide comfort, peace, and eternal life.

"Sometimes changing the world means getting quiet enough for God to change me." (Lysa Terkeurst)

Threads

John 4:1-42; James 1:2-4; 2 Corinthians 2:14

DAY 3

Peace of God

Philippians 4:6-7 (NLT)

Don't worry about anything; instead, pray about everything. Tell God what you need, and thank him for all he has done. Then you will experience God's peace, which exceeds anything we can understand. His peace will guard your hearts and minds as you live in Christ Jesus.

Blue Tassels

The Indianapolis Children's Museum is a place where I experienced both panic and peace.

We decided to take the kids to experience the museum. The youngest was six weeks old, our son was a little over two, and our older daughters were 6 and 8. We now realize how brave (and not too smart) we were in tackling the outing for the day.

We were taking a break on the lower level by the restrooms. I was seeing to the baby's needs and suddenly I realized our son was nowhere in sight. A bit of panic set in as we began calling out his name and looking for him. I stayed put in case he returned and my husband and others looked for him, up and down a spiral ramp, and back again.

A woman came out of the restroom and asked if I had a little boy. Yes! He had been in the restroom just watching the women come in and out, washing their hands. He must have thought I was in there; I don't know.

What I do know is that his curiosity turned to my fear, which turned to panic. Upon finding him (just a few feet away), tears of relief came freely, and peace ensued. (However, I said we were leaving and never coming back!)

I'm sure we prayed to find him, but I also worried we wouldn't. Believe me, when he was found, we were so thankful to God that he wasn't injured or abducted.

TASSEL OF PEACE

Have we had times of doubt, complaining, or not trusting that God had our back? Do we tend toward worry, temptation, arguing, or slander? None of these provide peace.

We need to turn our eyes to Jesus, who can give us forgiveness, mercy, grace, joy, rest, and peace.

Threads

*Proverbs 3:5; Philippians 3:13-14;
1 Peter 5:7; 1 John 1:9*

TASSEL OF PEACE

DAY 4

A Path of Peace

John 16:33

I HAVE TOLD YOU these things, so that in me you may have peace. In this world you will have trouble. But take heart! I have overcome the world.

Blue Tassels

In June 2022, I retired after 24.5 years of working as a paraprofessional in a transitional program for disabled young adults ages 18-21.

In my earlier years, I was with a beautiful young woman who was bound to a wheelchair due to a head injury suffered in a car collision involving a drunk driver. The community of her family, friends, and church rallied around her in prayer and assistance.

I learned so much from her peaceful attitude.

So many times we shared laughter, and my favorite was when she would look up from her wheelchair and say to me, "Deb, you rock, but I roll!"

She had such a gentle, loving spirit about her. She loved the Lord, smiled all the time, and his peace exuded from her. She was in trouble with her health, but God protected her and gave her a wonderful world of daily peace.

"God's peace is what we need most also. And we find His peace in His presence. God's presence can remove the clutter of fear and discouragement. It makes a path of peace for us to walk when we need to press through discouragement and courageously trust and serve Him in whatever ways He calls us to. His presence assures us that we are not alone, forsaken, or abandoned."*

God has told us we will have trouble in our lives. If you have not already experienced it, I'm thankful, but am sure there will be pain and trouble headed your way sometime. I am praying you have a relationship with our Lord Jesus Christ and have a prayerful, trustworthy, and gentle community from which you can draw strength and peace.

The Lord promises peace.

* Jennifer Rothschild, *66 Ways God Loves You* (Nashville: Thomas Nelson, 2016), 119

Blue Tassels

Threads

Isaiah 9:6-7; Isaiah 54:10; Matthew 5:9

Sharing the Tassel of Peace

John 14:25-27

"ALL THIS I HAVE spoken while still with you. But the Advocate, the Holy Spirit, whom the Father will send in my name, will teach you all things, and will remind you of everything I have said to you. Peace I leave with you; my peace I give you. I do not give to you as the world gives. Do not let your hearts be troubled and do not be afraid."

Blue Tassels

Jesus spoke these words to comfort his disciples not very long before he was arrested, tried, and crucified. He left his disciples with peace; the only one who could leave this peace.

To share the faith that we have involves action. If we send others off, wishing them peace without helping with their needs, what good is our faith? If we take action and see that their needs are met, we produce peace in their lives. James 3:18 says, "Peacemakers who sow in peace reap a harvest of righteousness."

How can we share this tassel of peace with others? The same way all of the tassels throughout this devotional have been shared.

Show compassion for struggling "neighbors". Shout about the hope that lives within you. Use the strength the Lord provided you to help others be strong. Comfort others with the comfort you have received from God. Radiate his love and reflect the relationship you have with your Lord. Love God, love yourself, and love others. Dress in clothes of forgiveness, not only for yourself, but for others as Christ forgave you. Do not hide your light, but share the rest offered to you by Jesus.

Rest in him. Peace to you.

Threads

*Romans 8:6; Ephesians 4:1-6;
James 2:14-17; James 3:13-18*

Afterword

WHILE HE WAS STILL *speaking to her, messengers arrived from the home of Jairus, the leader of the synagogue. They told him, "Your daughter is dead. There's no use troubling the Teacher now."*

But Jesus overheard them and said to Jairus, "Don't be afraid. Just have faith."

Then Jesus stopped the crowd and wouldn't let anyone go with him except Peter, James, and John (the brother of James). When they came to the home of the synagogue leader, Jesus saw much commotion and weeping and wailing. He went inside and asked, "Why all this commotion and weeping? The child isn't dead; she's only asleep."

The crowd laughed at him. But he made them all leave, and he took the girl's father and mother and his three disciples into the room where the girl was lying. Holding her hand, he said to her, "Talitha koum," which means "Little girl, get up!" And the girl, who was twelve years old, immediately stood up and walked around! They were overwhelmed and totally amazed. Jesus gave them strict orders not to tell anyone what had happened, and then he told them to give her something to eat. (Mark 5:35-43 NLT)

In literary terms, we have every reason to believe that, outside of Jesus, Jairus is the main character in this story. It is his urgent request that gets Jesus and the crowd moving through the narrow streets of Capernaum. His story opens and closes the section.

And yet, here we are at the tail end of a whole book about someone who, if they were casting a movie of it all, would barely be considered a supporting actress.

In the acting community, there's an oft-recited phrase that's meant to inflate the importance of each person's contribution to a performance (and keep everyone's ego in check): *There are no small roles, only small actors.* But in the Kingdom of God, there aren't even any small actors. Each person, no matter how insignificant they may seem in the estimation of a dog-eat-dog world, is cherished by their creator.

So if you feel like the hem-touching woman you've just spent 45 days with, take heart. No matter what Important Stuff you think Jesus cares about more than you, he is eager to look you in the eyes and say, "Your faith has made you well. Go in peace."

And if you identify with Jairus, anxiously hoping Jesus would hurry up and help you, take heart.

It may seem like he's letting himself get distracted with minor things (compared to what you need him for), but in the end, his timing is always best. "We know that God causes everything to work together for the good of those who love God and are called according to his purpose for them." (Romans 8:28 NLT)

> *Dewey Roth*
> *Husband of Debbie and author of the blog,*
> *Truth Is . . .*
> *https://deweytruth.blogspot.com*
> *April 2024*

Philippians 4:8-9

Finally, brothers and sisters, whatever is true, whatever is noble, whatever is right, whatever is pure, whatever is lovely, whatever is admirable—if anything is excellent or praiseworthy—think about such things. Whatever you have learned or received or heard from me, or seen in me—put it into practice. And the God of peace will be with you.

A Tassel of Thanks

Amy Walker Buchs—Thank you for letting me use your painting as the cover for this book. Watching photos of your creation process, turning the side of a small barn into a beautiful piece of art, was the seed that grew into these devotions.

Greg and Nancy Koomler—Thank you for allowing Amy to work her magic on your barn, and for paving the way for me to talk with her.

Patrick Redmond and Ray Steup—Getting a high-quality photo of Amy's work under time pressure spelled the difference between "okay" and "amazing" for this book's cover. Thank you.

Dewey Roth—Editing is just one of your many talents. Thanks for giving me the family discount.

About the Author

DEBBIE ROTH IS THE founder of Rest in Him Ministry as well as a singer, speaker, author, wife, mother, and grandmother. She lives in Rosemount, Minnesota with her husband, Dewey, and dog, Marco.

Debbie began Rest in Him Ministry as a way to turn the miseries she has experienced in her life into a ministry of hope and restoration. She has been comforting others with the comfort she has received from God (2 Corinthians 1:3-4) at retreats, banquets, and worship services since 2005.

Also available by Debbie Roth

DRENCHED: Only Hope in the Storm

Combining stories from her journey with truths from God's word, Debbie maps a route to how you can
- recognize and acknowledge your pain;
- understand God's forgiveness, grace, and mercy;
- apply God's forgiveness to those who may never ask for yours;

- trust God's promises of comfort, peace, rest, and hope;
- be refreshed and enabled to truly worship God; and
- turn your misery into ministry

THE HOPE SERIES

Four CDs full of faith-filled songs of comfort, encouragement, worship, and hope. Also available on a single flash drive.
- only HOPE in the storm
- endless HOPE
- drenched in HOPE
- living letters of HOPE

To learn more, please visit
www.RestInHimMinistry.weebly.com or
www.womenspeakers.com/minnesota/
rosemount/speaker/debbie-roth
To contact Debbie, please email
Debbie@RestInHimMinistry.com

Made in the USA
Monee, IL
03 July 2024